E.B. White

Other titles in the Inventors and Creators series include:

E.B. White

Adam Woog

KIDHAVEN PRESS
An imprint of Thomson Gale, a part of The Thomson Corporation

Detroit • New York • San Francisco • San Diego • New Haven, Conn. • Waterville, Maine • London • Munich

Once again, this is for Leah. After all, she let me read E.B. White's books to her when she was nearly as little as Stuart himself.

LIBRARY OF CONGRESS CATALOGING-IN-PUBLICATION DATA

Woog, Adam, 1953–
  E.B. White / by Adam Woog.
    p. cm. — (Inventors and creators)
  Includes bibliographical references and index.
  ISBN 0-7377-2612-1 (alk. paper)
  1. White, E. B. (Elwyn Brooks), 1899—Juvenile literature. 2. Authors, American—20th century—Biography—Juvenile literature. 3. Children's stories—Authorship—Juvenile literature. I. Title. II. Series.
  PS3545.H5187Z97 2005
  818'.5209—dc22   2004016280

Printed in the United States of America

Contents

Some Writer!

E.B. White was (and still is) one of America's most famous writers. Adults love his essays and magazine pieces because they are funny, thoughtful, and beautifully written. White is best known, however, as a writer for children.

He wrote only three kids' books: *Stuart Little*, *Charlotte's Web*, and *The Trumpet of the Swan*. Each has become a classic. Children regularly vote for them as their favorite books of all time, and they have been translated into dozens of languages. Millions of adults and children have enjoyed them for decades.

A Complex Person

The man behind these famous books was a complex person. White had many characteristics that sometimes seemed to **contradict** each other. For example, he lived for years in New York City but was a farmer at heart. He loved the city's diversity and excitement, and he wrote for a magazine that symbolized its sophistication. But White was happiest on his farm in Maine. He preferred chores like baling hay or building fences over anything he could do in the city.

White was a loner who needed to spend time by himself. He was terrified of speaking in public, and he avoided large groups. But White also deeply loved his family and needed them nearby. He was unhappy if they were not.

White was nervous all his life, and sometimes he was sad for no special reason. Also, he worried about small or imaginary

E.B. White's children's books have become some of the most beloved stories of all time.

things. For example, in college he rode trolley cars every day, and he constantly worried that their brakes would fail. He knew that the chances of this were tiny, but still he was fearful.

Later in his life, many aspects of modern living depressed White. He lived through two terrible world wars, and he worried about the condition of the world. White felt that progress was not always a good thing, and he generally preferred old-fashioned tools to new technology.

"All That I Ever Hope to Say"

On the other hand, White was generally cheerful and friendly in person. He was always kind and gentle, especially with animals and children. Furthermore, White was endlessly curious about everything around him. And, despite his doubts, he was fond of much of what he saw. He once commented, "All that I ever hope to say in books is that I love the world."[1] This love affair with the world around him began when White was very young.

Chapter One

Growing Up

Elwyn Brooks White was born on July 11, 1899, in Mount Vernon, New York. His parents were Samuel and Jessie White. The Whites were comfortably **affluent**, and they lived in a big, rambling house on a quiet street.

Samuel White was an executive in a piano company. He was a neat dresser, full of energy, and always curious about things. (Years later, Stuart Little had these same characteristics.)

Jessie White was kind, intelligent, and soft-spoken, and she loved animals and flowers. Like most women of her time, she did not work outside the home. However, she was busy, even with a maid and a cook to help, because Elwyn was the youngest of six children. The others were Marion, Clara, Albert, Stanley, and Lillian.

The Whites were a close family. Samuel and Jessie encouraged their children to learn and explore. They organized many family trips and outings to places like museums. Everyone played music, and the White home was filled with several pianos and other instruments.

A young E.B. White (front, center) is photographed with his mother Jessie (front, left) and four of his five siblings.

Everyone played something. Elwyn played piano, mandolin, and cello. He remarked years later, "We were practically a ready-made band. All we lacked was talent."[2]

At School

Elwyn, who was nicknamed En, attended public school, although he resisted going to kindergarten. He did not want to leave the safety and comfort of his family and home. Also, he was bored at school because he could already read, which put him ahead of the other students.

As he grew older, En was still nervous and uncomfortable at school. He was especially scared of being called on to speak in front of other students. This fear stayed with the writer all his life.

Solitude

En had many friends in town, but he also liked **solitude**. There were many ways to spend time alone. For instance, En spent hours playing with, watching, and caring for his pets. At various times, he kept dogs, chickens, lizards, ducks, and turkeys. En also liked to examine his large collection of bird eggs.

En especially loved the sights, sounds, and smells of the horse stable behind his house. He spent hours there watching the horses and talking with the man who drove the family's horse carriage. The birds, mice, and other small animals in the stable also fascinated the boy.

As a child, E.B. White spent much of his free time alone, with his pets and other animals.

En loved the outdoors. In cold weather he skated, hiked, and sledded. When it was warm, he sailed, canoed, and fished. A high point of every year for him was the Whites' month-long summer vacation at a lake in Maine.

Early Writing

En's first writing, which began when he was about seven, was a journal of things he saw and did. He also wrote down his thoughts, which were often about nature. He wondered why foxes bark and how birds know when to build nests. Many years later, White used some of this journal to create Sam Beaver's journal in *The Trumpet of the Swan*.

En's writing was published for the first time when he was eleven. A popular magazine for kids, *St. Nicholas*, printed one of his stories. *St. Nicholas* later published more of them, and two stories won prizes.

The boy always liked forming his ideas into written words. He later recalled: "I can't remember any time in my life when I wasn't busy writing. I don't know what caused me to do it, or why I enjoyed it, but I think children often find pleasure and satisfaction in trying to set their thoughts down on paper, either in words or in pictures. I was no good at drawing, so I used words instead."[3]

A Disastrous Date

In high school, En got good grades and helped edit the school's literary magazine, but it was not an especially happy time for him. He was slender and

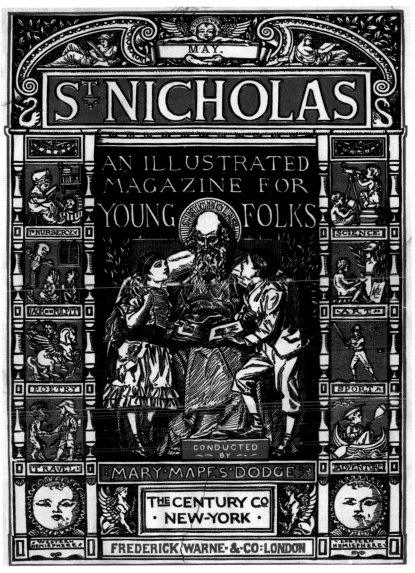

When E.B. was only eleven one of his stories was published in *St. Nicholas*, a popular children's magazine.

suffered from allergies, so he did not play school sports. He was also still terrified of public speaking.

En was shy around girls, too. He never knew what to say to them. Finally, he worked up his courage to ask one girl, Eileen Thomas, on a date. He carefully planned their afternoon, wanting to make it perfect.

Unfortunately, the plan was too complicated. Instead of doing something simple like going to a local show, En took Eileen on a train to New York City. They were too shy to say much to each other.

Then they went dancing. En did not like to dance, but he thought Eileen would. They drank some tea and came home, still too shy to talk much. This unsuccessful afternoon later inspired Stuart Little's date with Harriet Ames, which also was ruined by being too complicated.

Cornell

In 1917, En entered Cornell University, a well-known school in Ithaca, New York. Both of his brothers had gone there. En's classmates gave him a new name:

At Cornell University, E.B., or Andy as his friends called him, developed his writing skills while working for the school newspaper.

Andy. Friends called him Andy for the rest of his life. He had always disliked Elwyn and joked, "My mother just hung it on me because she'd run out of names. I was her sixth child."[4]

Andy liked college, but he was not a straight-A student. Instead of studying, he spent his time working on the school paper, the *Daily Sun*. He was a reporter and, later, editor.

Although he was still shy, Andy did have a girlfriend at college. She was Alice Burchfield, a student in the drama department. He wrote her many romantic poems.

From Camp Counselor to Jobholder

For two summers during college, Andy was a counselor at Camp Otter, a boy's camp in Canada. He used some of his experiences there to invent Camp Kookooskoos in *The Trumpet of the Swan*. For example, while he was at camp, Andy wrote many love-struck letters to Alice. This romantic mood is re-created when Louis the swan **courts** Serena.

Also, the story of Louis rescuing a camper from drowning is based on a real episode. Andy and another counselor saved a boy who became seriously ill on a wilderness trip. They canoed all night to get him to safety.

When Andy graduated from Cornell in 1921, he took several jobs related to reporting, but he never stayed with them for long. For example, he was hired to edit news bulletins and send them all over the country. The job was unsatisfying because it was not creative. Andy quit after only a month.

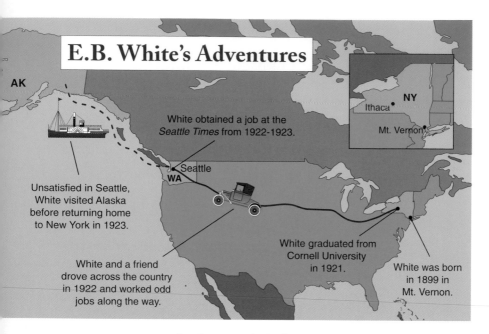

E.B. White's Adventures

AK

NY

Ithaca

Mt. Vernon

White obtained a job at the *Seattle Times* from 1922-1923.

Seattle
WA

Unsatisfied in Seattle, White visited Alaska before returning home to New York in 1923.

White and a friend drove across the country in 1922 and worked odd jobs along the way.

White graduated from Cornell University in 1921.

White was born in 1899 in Mt. Vernon.

A Grand Adventure

Tired of looking for work, Andy set off on a grand adventure. He and Howard Cushman, a friend who also wanted to become a writer, drove across the United States. Their car was loaded down with camping equipment and car repair tools—as well as typewriters, books, and other things the young writers needed. As they traveled, the friends worked at odd jobs such as baling hay or packing fruit.

In Seattle, Washington, Howard decided to go home, but Andy found a job at the *Seattle Times*. However, Seattle's gray weather depressed him. After nine months, Andy took a boat to Alaska, just because he had always wanted to see it. Then, eighteen months after he left, Andy White went home.

Chapter Two

Stuart Little Is Born

White was still determined to become a writer. He and three Cornell friends shared an apartment in Manhattan. White sold poems and other pieces to newspapers and magazines, including a new magazine called the *New Yorker*.

White's blend of gentle humor and sharp observation perfectly suited this magazine. Its publisher asked White to become a staff writer, but he resisted. He liked the freedom of being a **freelance** writer. The publisher kept after him, however, and in 1927 White joined the *New Yorker* full time.

Starting a Family

One of the first people White met there was Katharine Angell, the *New Yorker*'s fiction editor. Kay, as she was called, was intelligent, cultured, and beautiful. She also had an important career, unusual for a woman then.

The two fell in love and got married in 1929. Kay had two young children from a previous marriage, who continued to live with their father. Andy and Kay had a son together in 1930.

E.B. White and his wife Kay met while working at the *New Yorker*. The couple married in 1929.

Like many new parents, White was both delighted and terrified when his son Joel was born. Mostly, however, he enjoyed fatherhood. After his son's birth, White wrote a little poem in a letter to a friend: "Sex is male, color white, and a dandy son all right all right. First name Joel, then McCoun, and all in all he's such a boon."[5]

The Farm

As both a father and a writer, White loved living in New York. He liked the diversity and excitement that the city offered. But White also longed for a simpler, slower life in the country. He was happiest there, and he wanted to offer that life to his son. In 1933, he and Kay bought a farm on the coast of Maine, near the town of North Brooklin. It included forty acres of land and an old twelve-room house.

The farm was their home, off and on, for the rest of their lives. Sometimes the Whites spent only summers there, sometimes all year. Living in Maine let them

After moving to a farm in Maine, White wrote part-time for both *Harper's* and the *New Yorker*.

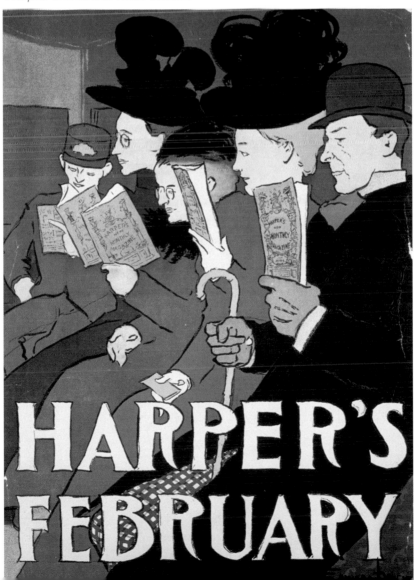

work just part-time, because their expenses were much less there than in New York City. Andy wrote for two magazines, the *New Yorker* and *Harper's*, and Kay edited fiction and reviewed children's books for the *New Yorker*. White remarked that farm life gave him enough time for "shingling a barn or sandpapering an old idea."[6]

The farm was home to sheep, chickens, and at least one dog, cat, and pig at any given time. At various times the Whites also kept cows and other large animals. In addition, there were many wild animals nearby, such as birds, foxes, and deer.

Much of White's day was spent with animals. It was natural that they would find their way into his writing. He once commented, "I like animals, and it would be odd if I failed to write about them."[7]

Stuart Is Born

White was very good at closely observing animals. This helped him create characters that acted, in many ways, just like real ones. For example, in *Charlotte's Web*, Charlotte spins her web in the same way, and for the same reasons, as a real spider.

The first animal White wrote about was a mouse named Stuart. Stuart was born one night when White was asleep on a train. The writer dreamed of a tiny, well-dressed, brave, and adventurous figure with the features of a mouse. White later wrote, "When I woke up . . . I made a few notes about this mouse-child—the only fictional figure ever to have honored and disturbed my sleep."[8]

White named this creature Stuart Little and made up some stories about him to amuse the children he knew. These tales were about a boy who looks like, and is as big as, a mouse. He is born into an otherwise normal human family, the Littles. Although the Littles are surprised, they accept and love Stuart. He has many thrilling adventures, such as racing on a toy boat and sliding down a drain to find his mother's jewelry.

E.B. White created the character Stuart Little, after the adventurous mouse appeared in one of his dreams.

While living in Manhattan in 1944, White decided to make Stuart's stories into a book. America was in the middle of World War II, and White had been writing about it for the *New Yorker*. Stuart was a welcome break from the sad, serious subject of war.

Many details about Stuart came from White's own life. For example, both Stuart and his creator loved boats and cars. Both were smart, funny, and good at fixing things. Both liked to be up before anyone else in the morning, when the air seemed fresh. And both had once carefully planned a date that went terribly wrong.

Controversy

White had already written several books for adults, and they were popular with both the public and critics. His editor for these books, Ursula Nordstrom, was concerned when White told her that he was writing for children. She knew that people who write well for adults do not always do the same for kids.

However, Nordstrom thought the **manuscript** of *Stuart Little* was wonderful. She later commented: "It was marvelously well-written, and funny, and touching. I loved the diminutive [tiny] hero, and I knew children would."[9]

Although Nordstrom liked it, *Stuart Little* upset at least one important adult: Anne Carroll Moore, the retired children's librarian at the New York Public Library. Moore strongly disliked *Stuart Little* when she saw the manuscript. She was bothered by

The imaginative character of Stuart Little shares many traits in common with White.

the idea of a woman giving birth to a tiny mouselike creature. She thought that it would confuse and frighten children.

Moore wrote Kay White a long letter, begging her not to let her husband ruin his reputation by publishing *Stuart Little*. White respected the librarian's opinion but disagreed. He felt that kids could handle such a flight of imagination: "Children can sail easily over the fence that separates reality from make-believe."[10]

Success

White was correct. When *Stuart Little* appeared in 1945, it was a big success. It sold well, and White was surprised that newspaper critics treated the book seriously. They reviewed it as though it were adult fiction. Nearly all of them praised it.

Not everyone was completely pleased, however. White commented later that some people were offended by his choice of names: "Three fellows turned up claiming that their name was Stuart Little, and what was I going to do about that? One of them told me he had begun work on a children's story: The hero was a rat and the rat's name was E.B. White."[11]

White was encouraged by the success of *Stuart Little*. He started thinking about a second book for kids. In time, this became a story about a pig and a spider.

Chapter Three

Charlotte and Louis

White's second book for children was *Charlotte's Web*. This book, probably his most famous, was inspired by an incident on White's farm. In 1948, White wrote a magazine essay, "Death of a Pig." It was about White failing to save a sick pig. White was filled with grief when he was unable to rescue the animal from death.

The experience gave him an idea for a story about saving a pig. He then added another animal: "I had been watching a big grey spider at her work and was impressed by how clever she was at weaving. Gradually I worked the spider into the story. . . . Three years after I started writing it, it was published. (I am not a fast worker, as you can see.)"[12]

White's story became a tale of friendship between a pig, Wilbur, and a spider, Charlotte A. Cavatica, who saves Wilbur from being butchered for meat. She does this by weaving words into webs above Wilbur's pen. The family that owns Wilbur thinks this is sort of a miracle, and when Wilbur wins a prize at the county fair they decide to keep him. Wilbur is later able to repay the favor, protecting Charlotte's eggs so her children can grow.

Creating Charlotte

It took White a long time to find the right way to tell his story. He joked in a letter to his editor that the manuscript was growing very slowly: "I look at it every day. I keep it in a carton, as you would a kitten."[13]

Charlotte the spider, Wilbur the pig, and all of the characters of *Charlotte's Web* were inspired by real events in White's life.

One reason it took so long was that White rewrote most of it several times before he was satisfied. For example, he changed the opening chapter completely. Originally, it started with a long description of the barn where Wilbur lived. But this was not very exciting, so he opened the book with Fern, the farmer's daughter, discovering that a pig was about to be killed.

Another reason why it took so long was that White needed to do a lot of research. He wanted his story to remain true to how spiders or pigs would really act. He spent a whole year studying spiders. He read everything he could about them and carefully watched a particular spider in his Maine barn.

Episodes from Life

Once again, White based parts of *Charlotte's Web* on his own life. For instance, every summer in Maine the Whites attended a county fair, the Blue Hill Fair. In 1946, Joel, then a teenager, took his girlfriend for a ride on the Ferris Wheel. The fair and the Ferris Wheel became important parts of White's book.

A special moment in *Charlotte's Web* comes when Wilbur rescues Charlotte's **egg sac**. It was inspired by a real incident. In his barn, White watched his spider (also called Charlotte) as she spun an egg sac and deposited her eggs in it. When he returned to New York, White did not want to leave the spider behind.

He carefully cut the sac away from the barn wall, put Charlotte and her sac in a box, and brought them

White's real-life fascination with a spider that spun an egg sac in his barn produced one of the most memorable moments in *Charlotte's Web*.

to the city. White put the box on his bedroom dresser. He recalled:

> Some weeks later I was surprised and pleased to find that Charlotte's daughters were emerging from the air holes in the cover of the box. They strung tiny lines from my comb to my brush, from my brush to my mirror, and from my mirror

to my nail scissors. They were very busy and almost invisible, they were so small. We all lived together happily for a couple of weeks and then somebody whose duty it was to dust my dresser balked, and I broke up the show.[14]

Louis

White had already proven he could write for kids, and this time there was no controversy or doubt. When *Charlotte's Web* came out in 1952, the reviews were glowing and it was an immediate bestseller. However, White waited almost twenty years, until

Through music and writing, Louis, the mute hero of *The Trumpet of the Swan,* finds his voice.

1970, to publish *The Trumpet of the Swan*, his third book for children.

Louis, the hero of this story, is a beautiful trumpeter swan. But Louis has a problem: He is **mute**. He cannot make sounds to communicate with other swans. However, Louis learns to communicate in two ways. One is writing, which a young boy, Sam Beaver, teaches him. The other is playing a trumpet that Louis's father steals by smashing the window of a music store. Louis uses his trumpet to make money and repay the store. The trumpet also helps him win the heart of Serena, a beautiful female swan.

With help from his friend Sam Beaver, Louis the swan learns to communicate through writing.

White could not pinpoint what inspired him to create this story. He wrote: "I don't know how or when the idea . . . occurred to me. I guess I must have wondered what it would be like to be a Trumpeter Swan and not be able to make a noise."[15]

More Research

Once again, White researched his subject thoroughly. For example, he asked his old friend Howard Cushman to visit some newly hatched swans at the zoo in Philadelphia, Cushman's home. White wanted Cushman to observe them closely and report all the details back.

He also relied on his own memory. For example, he recalled watching a loon (another waterbird) sitting on a nest with a day-old chick and an unhatched egg. And White again used his own life as inspiration.

For example, Louis's muteness reflected White's own fear of speaking in public. Like Louis, White communicated best by writing—even with Kay, to whom he sometimes wrote long letters when he needed to say something important. According to biographer Scott Elledge, White used elements of himself to create both of the book's main characters: "There is some of Andy in Louis as well as in Sam Beaver."[16]

By the time *The Trumpet of the Swan* was published, White had for years been considered one of America's most important writers. Now, as he grew older, he began to receive many honors and awards.

Chapter Four

A Quiet End to a Long Life

Many of the awards and honors White received were for his kids' books. For example, he won the Laura Ingalls Wilder Medal. This is one of the most important honors in children's literature.

Other awards were for his writing for adults. For instance, he received the Presidential Medal of Freedom, the highest honor the United States gives to civilians. White also received a Pulitzer Prize, a Gold Medal from the National Institute of Arts and Letters, the National Medal for Literature, and many more. Furthermore, White was given honorary degrees from seven colleges and universities.

Charlotte's Web was made into an animated movie in 1973, but White did not like it very much. To him the characters seemed unrealistic, and he thought the songs were weak. He wrote to a friend: "The story is interrupted every few minutes so that somebody can sing a jolly song. I don't care much for jolly songs."[17]

No Travel

The writer appreciated receiving honors, but he almost never traveled to accept them in person. In part, this was because he had always hated ceremonies and public speaking. Furthermore, White disliked travel in general. Starting in 1957, the Whites had lived in Maine full-time, partly so they could avoid the tiring trip up from New York City. Another reason was that the Whites could be near Joel and his own family. Joel had become a boat designer and builder in North Brooklin. He was married and had children, and Andy and Kay loved spending time with them.

E.B. White works at his typewriter in his office at the *New Yorker*. His children's books earned him many awards.

During the last years of his life, White preferred to spend time on his farm playing with his grandchildren.

Except for short trips into North Brooklin, where he was involved in local projects like the library, White rarely left the farm at all during this period. When he did, it was usually not successful. For instance, a magazine asked him to travel across America by car. He was to report on how things had changed since his own journey in the 1920s. White got as far as Pennsylvania before turning back. He hated the speed of the freeways and was saddened at how different things were.

A Man of Regular Habits

On the farm, White had regular habits. He usually got up at 6:00 A.M. and started the wood fire in the kitchen stove. Then he did morning chores, such as feeding the animals. For the rest of the morning, he wrote.

White wrote in a notebook with a pen, or he used an old typewriter. Sometimes, he worked in his study in the main house. When possible, though, he liked to work in the boathouse by the water. This was a small building, 10 feet (3m) by 15 feet (4.6m) —about the size of a typical bedroom. It was heated by a woodstove and contained only a chair, a wooden table, a bench, and a wastebasket made from an old keg. Its one window looked out on White's beloved sea.

In the afternoons, if there were no other chores, White liked to sail. His boat was a 19-foot sloop (5.8m) called *Martha*, named for his granddaughter. White's son Joel built *Martha* to replace a larger boat, *Fern*, that the writer had owned.

White had to replace his old boat because he was having physical problems such as **arthritis**, and *Fern* was too big to sail by himself. This change of boats was one way in which White admitted he was slowing down, although he jokingly commented that he always thought of himself as "a lad of about 19."[18]

Illness and Death

As he got older, White's health problems worsened. All his life, the writer had worried about his health. He suffered from hay fever and other allergies. Also, he had stomach pains every time he had to appear in front of an audience.

But White was also a **hypochondriac**, someone who worries a lot about personal health. For instance, a simple cough in college had become, in his mind, a serious, life-threatening disease called tuberculosis. On another occasion, a sunburn on his forehead somehow convinced White that he had a brain tumor. Now, his health really was poor. He had problems with his heart, his eyes, and his joints.

White's beloved wife was in even worse health. The writer tenderly nursed Kay for years until her death in 1977.

White was so grief stricken that he could not go to his wife's funeral. As always, he expressed his feelings best through writing. He wrote words that other family members spoke at Kay's memorial service. Later, he planted an oak tree near Kay's grave to honor her memory.

The writer was deeply depressed after Kay's death. She had been his constant companion and great friend for nearly fifty years. After her death, he commented, "Life without Katharine is no good for me."[19]

Death of an Author

The writer appeared even less frequently in public. He resisted giving interviews and rarely answered fan mail. He discouraged visitors, even old friends, and he tried to keep away the many fans who arrived, usually unannounced, in search of those imaginary animals Charlotte and Wilbur. Nonetheless, White continued to work. Among the books he

Although it was published more than half a century ago, *Charlotte's Web* is a favorite among children to this day.

published during this time were a book of letters and one of essays and poems.

White died at home on October 1, 1985, at the age of 86. He was buried next to his wife in North Brooklin. Friends and fans all over the world mourned the writer's passing.

Luckily for children all over the world, White's creations did not die with him. His books remain as popular as ever, and all have been made into movies. Two movies about Stuart Little, combining live action and computer graphics, were made after White's death. Meanwhile, a new version of *Charlotte's Web* is scheduled for 2006.

E.B. White is remembered for the lovable characters he created for his inspired children's stories.

White's books remain popular partly because they are exciting stories. But they are more than that. They are also tender, funny, and fresh books with important themes such as loyalty, friendship, and **tolerance**.

White could convey these themes by having his animals act like humans. Some, such as Templeton the rat, are mean or selfish. They are sometimes sad or short-tempered, as Stuart Little sometimes is. But they can also be kind, loving, and generous—Charlotte, Wilbur, and Louis are just three examples.

White's animals are just as good or bad as humans are, and they tell readers something about human nature. He once wrote:

> In real life, a family doesn't have a child who looks like a mouse; in real life, a spider doesn't spin words in her web. In real life, a swan doesn't blow a trumpet. But real life is only one kind of life—there is also the life of the imagination. And although my stories are imaginary, I like to think that there is some truth in them, too—truth about the way people and animals feel and think and act.[20]

Notes

Introduction: Some Writer!

1. Quoted in Robert van Gelder, "The Author of 'One Man's Meat' Talks About Writing and Country Living." www.nytimes.com/books/97/08/03/lifetimes/white-interview.html.

Chapter One: Growing Up

2. E.B. White, *Letters of E.B. White.* New York: Harper & Row, 1976, p. 3.

3. Quoted in E.B. White Official Home Page. www.harperchildrens.com/authorintro/index.asp?authorid=10499.

4. Quoted in Herbert Mitgang, "E.B. White, Essayist and Stylist, Dies," *New York Times*, October 2, 1985. www.nytimes.com/learning/general/onthisday/bday/0711.html.

Chapter Two: Stuart Little Is Born

5. White, *Letters of E.B. White.*, p. 102.

6. White, *Letters of E.B. White.*, p. 180.

7. Quoted in Scott Elledge, *E.B. White: A Biography.* New York: W.W. Norton, 1984, p. 289.

8. Quoted in Elledge, *E.B. White*, p. 253.

9. Ursula Nordstrom, "Stuart, Wilbur, Charlotte: A

Tale of Tales," *New York Times*, May 12, 1974. www.nytimes.com/books/97/08/03/lifetimes/whitetales.html.

10. Quoted in Elledge, *E.B. White*, p. 264.

11. Quoted in van Gelder, "The Author of 'One Man's Meat' Talks About Writing and Country Living."

Chapter Three: Charlotte and Louis

12. Quoted in E.B. White Official Home Page.

13. White, *Letters of E.B. White*, p. 314.

14. Quoted in Elledge, *E.B. White*, p. 294.

15. Quoted in E.B. White Official Home Page.

16. Elledge, *E.B. White*, p. 64.

Chapter Four: A Quiet End to a Long Life

17. White, *Letters of E.B. White*, p. 646.

18. Quoted in Elledge, *E.B. White*, pp. 349–50.

19. Quoted in Mitgang, "E.B. White, Essayist and Stylist, Dies."

20. Quoted in E.B. White Official Home Page.

Glossary

affluent: Well-off, with enough money to be comfortable.

arthritis: A disease that affects the joints, making them stiff and painful. Arthritis is typically suffered by some people as they get older.

contradict: To go against or be the opposite of something.

courts: Romantically pursues or seeks favor.

egg sac: The protective container that some animals (such as spiders) make for their eggs.

freelance: Independent, being one's own boss.

hypochondriac: Someone who worries about health too much and is convinced that even tiny illnesses are serious.

manuscript: The text of a book when it is sent from the writer to the publisher.

mute: Unable to make a sound.

solitude: Time spent alone, away from the company of others.

tolerance: The ability to understand and accept things that are different or new.

For Further Exploration

Books About E.B. White

David R. Collins, *To the Point: A Story About E.B. White*. Minneapolis, MN: Carolrhoda, 1989. This nicely written biography, written for slightly older students, concentrates on White's life as a whole rather than on his children's books.

Cynthia Rylant, *Margaret, Frank, & Andy: Three Writers' Stories*. New York: Harcourt, Brace, 1996. A short but sweet book about three beloved children's book writers: Margaret Wise Brown, L. Frank Baum, and E.B. White.

S. Ward, *Meet E.B. White*. New York: PowerKids, 2001. A very simple and busily illustrated book about White.

Books by E.B. White

E.B. White, *Charlotte's Web*. New York: HarperTrophy, 1974. A paperback edition of White's most famous book, illustrated by Garth Williams.

E.B. White, *Stuart Little*. New York: HarperTrophy, 1974. This paperback edition of White's first book for kids has charming illustrations by Garth Williams.

E.B. White, *The Trumpet of the Swan*. New York: HarperTrophy, 2000. Illustrated by Fred Marcellino, this is a paperback of White's third book for children.

Web Sites

Charlotte's Web (www.2.lhric.org/pocantico/charlotte). A fun Web site created by a second-grade class in Sleepy Hollow, New York, with poems, crossword puzzles, and many other things devoted to the book.

E.B. White Official Home Page (www.harperchildrens. com/authorintro/index.asp?authorid=10499). This site is maintained by White's longtime publisher.

Stuart Little 2 (www.sonypictures.com/movies/ stuartlittle). A site with games and other activities devoted to the sequel to the movie version of White's famous book.

Index

Picture Credits

About the Author

Adam Woog grew up in Seattle, Washington, and lives there now with his family. He has written many books for adults, young adults, and children. Woog is also a longtime contributor to the *Seattle Times*, where E.B. White was once a reporter.